The Ancient Romans

ROSEMARY REES

Heinemann Library
Chicago, Illinois

© 1999 Reed Educational & Professional Publishing
Published by Heinemann Library,
an imprint of Reed Educational & Professional Publishing,
Chicago, IL

Customer Service 888-454-2279

Visit our website at www.heinemannlibrary.com

Designed by Julian Holland Publishing
Artwork by Martin Smillie
Printed in Hong Kong

05 04 03
10 9 8 7 6 5 4 3

Library of Congress Cataloging-in-Publication Data
Rees, Rosemary, 1942-
    The ancient Romans / Rosemary Rees.
      p. cm. – (Understanding people in the past)
    Summary: Examines the social, economic, political, and cultural
life of the ancient Romans. Sidebars describe specific statues,
murals, and ruins of the period.
    Includes bibliographical references and index.
    ISBN 1-57572-890-7 (lib. bdg.)   ISBN 1-58810-316-1 (pbk. bdg.)
    1. Rome—Civilization—Juvenile literature. 2. Rome—Antiquities-
–Pictorial works—Juvenile literature. [1. Rome—Civilization.
2. Rome—Antiquities.] I. Title. II. Series.
DG78.R44   1999
937-dc21   98-43260
                                                       CIP
                                                       AC

Acknowledgments
The author and publisher are grateful to the following for permission to reproduce copyright material:

Cover photograph © Art Resource/Erich Lessing

R. Agache, p. 24; Ancient Art and Architecture Collection, pp. 5 top, 6 top, 8 left and right, 9 top, 12 bottom, 13, 14 bottom, 19, 21, 22 top, 23 top, 30, 33 right, 35 top, 38 left, 40, 42, 45 top and bottom, 49, 50 right, 51, 52 bottom, 55, 56 top, 59; British Museum, p. 16 left; C.M. Dixon, pp. 5 bottom, 10, 26 top, 31 left, 35 bottom; Sonia Halliday Photographs, pp. 6 bottom, 38 right; Michael Holford, title page, pp. 7, 14 top, 15, 16 top, 23 bottom, 31 right and left, 36, 39, 41, 43 top and bottom, 46, 47, 54, 56 bottom, 57, 58; Hulton Picture Company, p 52 top; Museum of London/Jan Sorivener, pp. 9 bottom, 34; Mansell Collection, pp. 12 top, 17, 20, 50 left; Picturepoint, p. 28; Scala, p. 18; Trustees of the National Museums of Scotland, p. 27; Reg Wilson, p. 53.

Every effort has been made to contact copyright holders of any material reproduced in this book. Any omissions will be rectified in subsequent printings if notice is given to the publisher.

Some words are shown in bold, **like this.** You can find out what they mean by looking in the glossary.

Contents

Who Were the Romans?

Between 2000 and 1000 B.C., people from central Asia began moving into the country we now call Italy. One group settled by the Tiber River. The people farmed the flat land by the river. They traded with other settlers. They built villages on the seven hilltops surrounding their settlement. These villages became the city of Rome.

Kings

The Romans chose their kings. Lucius Tarquinius was the seventh and last king of Rome. He was cruel and unpopular. In 510 B.C., the Romans drove him out.

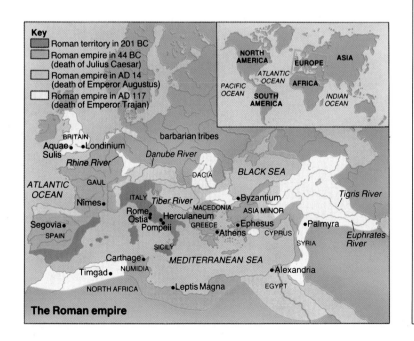

Key
- Roman territory in 201 BC
- Roman empire in 44 BC (death of Julius Caesar)
- Roman empire in AD 14 (death of Emperor Augustus)
- Roman empire in AD 117 (death of Emperor Trajan)

NORTH AMERICA, EUROPE, ASIA, ATLANTIC OCEAN, AFRICA, PACIFIC OCEAN, SOUTH AMERICA, INDIAN OCEAN

BRITAIN, Aquae Sulis, Londinium, barbarian tribes, Danube River, Rhine River, DACIA, BLACK SEA, ATLANTIC OCEAN, GAUL, Nîmes, ITALY, Tiber River, Rome, Ostia, Herculaneum, Pompeii, MACEDONIA, ASIA MINOR, GREECE, Byzantium, Ephesus, Athens, CYPRUS, Palmyra, Tigris River, Segovia, SPAIN, SICILY, SYRIA, Euphrates River, Carthage, NUMIDIA, MEDITERRANEAN SEA, Timgad, Leptis Magna, NORTH AFRICA, EGYPT, Alexandria

The Roman empire

B.C. and A.D.
Each year has a number. These numbers, or dates, count the years before and after the year Jesus Christ was born. Dates before the birth of Christ have the letters *B.C.* written after them, for example, 2000 B.C. B.C. stands for "before Christ." Remember that 1000 B.C. is closer in time to us than 2000 B.C. Dates after the birth of Christ have the letters *A.D.* written in front of them, for example, A.D. 900. A.D. stands for *Anno Domini*. These words mean "in the year of our Lord" in the Latin language.
The Romans divided their year into months to match changes in the moon. Their year had 355 days, and the months slowly got out of step with the seasons. Julius Caesar started a new calendar. It had 365 days like the calendar used today.

Roman roads, bridges, and buildings can still be seen today. The Colosseum in Rome was finished in A.D. 80. It is 170 feet (52 meters) high and once held 50,000 people.

The republic

The Romans set up a **republic** in 509 B.C. They still chose their leader, but only for a fixed time. Then they chose a new one. Rome was a republic for 500 years. The Romans became powerful and conquered other lands, including Greece.

The empire

In 27 B.C., the Romans made Augustus their first **emperor**. He ruled over Rome and all the lands conquered by the Romans. He was the ruler of more than 60 million people.

For 300 years, the Romans spread their skills and knowledge throughout their **empire**.

This wall painting is from a house in the town of Pompeii. It is about 2,000 years old. Experts think it is a picture of the owner of the house and his wife.

How Do We Know About the Romans?

Archaeologists have uncovered clues about the Romans. They dig in the ground and excavate buried objects. They find pottery, jewelry, and household objects. These objects give clues about how the Romans lived. They also find graves. Objects buried with the dead tell about their religious beliefs. Sometimes archaeologists uncover entire buildings, towns, and cities.

In A.D. 79, the volcano Vesuvius erupted. Hot ash and mud buried the cities of Herculaneum and Pompeii. Clues to these two cities were found accidentally.

Archaeologists carefully uncover everything they find.

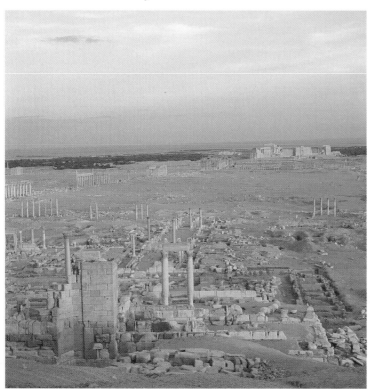

Some ancient Roman buildings can still be seen. This is Palmyra in the desert of Syria, in the Middle East.

6

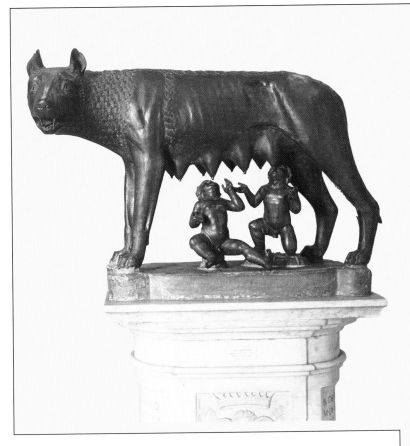

Legend or Fact?
A Roman legend tells how Rome began. Romulus and Remus were twin brothers. Their wicked uncle threw the babies into the Tiber River. But they didn't drown. A she-wolf heard them crying. She looked after them until a shepherd found them. He and his wife raised the boys as if they were their own children.

When the twins grew up, they decided to build a city at the place where they were rescued. They began to build the city. But they quarreled, and Romulus killed Remus. The city of Rome, begun in 753 B.C., is named for Romulus, its first king.

In 1709, men digging a well found the Herculaneum **amphitheater**. Years later, a farmer who was plowing fields found the city of Pompeii.

In A.D. 365, Ammianus Marcellinus saw and wrote about an earthquake on Cyprus. Archaeologists followed the ancient written clues. In the 1970s, they found the Roman town of Kourion on Cyprus. It was the town that had been buried by that earthquake.

Books and letters

The Romans wrote books about their past. Livy, a historian, wrote 142 books on Roman history. The Romans wrote letters about their daily lives. Pliny the Younger wrote hundreds of letters to his friends. His letters tell about Roman life from A.D. 55 to 120.

Words on walls

Archaeologists found graffiti on walls in Pompeii. People wrote on walls then, just as they do today. Some graffiti said things about elections of town officials. "Vote for Julius Philippus and he'll do the same for you" was one slogan uncovered by archaeologists.

Sometimes the Romans wrote on papyrus. This is a type of paper made from reeds. Writing carved into stone can still be read today. Words on a tombstone, like this one, usually praise the dead person.

Latin

Latin was the official language of the Roman **Empire**. The conquered countries of the empire were expected to speak and read Latin. Latin still exists because it was the language of the Catholic Church. Church services were conducted in Latin.

This stone carving shows Roman clothes and hair styles. A lady is having her hair done. Her maids are helping her.

Words and images that last

Archaeologists have found important documents and certificates written on bronze. Bronze is a long-lasting metal.

Wall paintings also tell us much about everyday Roman life. Statues, sculptures, and carvings show how people looked.

Archaeologists have uncovered **mosaic** floors. The Romans made mosaics from small tiles of colored stone or pottery. When they laid the floors, they made pictures of Roman life using the colored stone.

9

Government

When Rome became a **republic** in 509 B.C., the people were determined that no one person should have too much power.

The **citizens** of Rome met in a group called a comita. There were four of these groups. Every year each comita elected **magistrates**. Their names were written on a board in the **forum**, which was the central meeting place in Rome. Magistrates had the power to enforce the law. The most powerful magistrates were the two **consuls**. They had to agree with each other because one consul could cancel, or veto, the other's decisions.

Women, slaves, and people not born in Rome were not citizens. This meant they could not vote to choose their leaders.

The forum was an open market square, or meeting place. The Romans built buildings around each side of the square. The Forum Romanum became the center of government. The first curia, or **Senate** house, was built in 670 B.C. This was where senators met to discuss problems. The basilicas were large halls used for banquets and law courts. Politicians spoke to the people from the rostra.

The Forum Romanum was also the center of religion. These remaining columns were part of the **Temple** of Castor and Pollux. Romans believed these gods helped them in battle.

The Forum Romanum
basilica Aemilia
basilica of Maxentius
temple
temple
temple
rostra
senate house or *curia*

Most magistrates also served as a member of the Senate for the rest of their lives. At different times, there were between 300 and 900 senators. They advised the consuls.

After 27 B.C., the Romans had an **emperor**. He chose the members of the Senate. He decided who would be the next emperor.

Each Roman territory, or **province**, was ruled by a governor. He ruled in the name of the people of Rome. The Senate, and later the emperor, chose the governors. They had usually served as magistrates in Rome.

People and the Law

Romans divided their citizens into two classes. **Patricians** were rich **nobles** who owned a lot of land. **Plebeians** were tradesmen, servants, and men with small farms. The patricians had more votes than the plebeians. Only patricians could become **magistrates** and senators.

But in 494 B.C., the plebeians had enough of this inequality. They threatened to leave Rome. The patricians agreed that the plebeians could choose two officers called **tribunes**. The tribunes had the power to veto actions of the magistrates or **consuls**. After 366 B.C., one consul was always a plebeian.

Slaves worked for nothing and were often badly treated by their owners. Many slaves worked in mines or on farms. The life of a household slave was easier. Slaves had no legal rights. They could not vote. Slaves could be freed when their masters died.

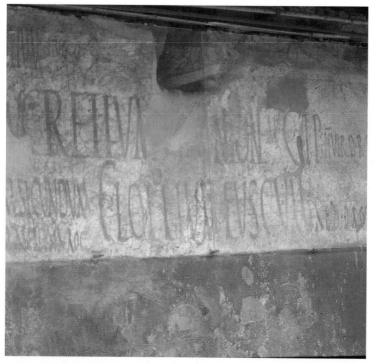

This writing is a political advertisement for public fights put on by Lucretius Satrus. He hoped that this entertainment would persuade people to vote for Quintus Postumus.

Roman law

Roman law began in the families. These rules were handed down from one family to another. Then kings made rules and passed judgments. When the Roman Republic began in 509 B.C., laws were not written. They were only spoken.

In 450 B.C., the laws of Rome were written on bronze tablets. Punishments were written there, too. They were displayed in the **forum** for everyone to see.

Over hundreds of years, new laws were made. In A.D. 529, the Emperor Justinian ordered all the laws to be written in a Code of Law. Today, many countries base their laws on the laws of ancient Rome.

Cicero

Marcus Tullius Cicero lived from 106 B.C. to 43 B.C. By 70 B.C., he was Rome's most important lawyer. He became a consul in 63 B.C.

Cicero wrote many speeches and letters about the people and politics of Rome. More than 900 of his letters have survived. He translated the work of Greek philosophers and he wrote books of his own. Many of his ideas came from the Greeks. His writings were used as text books in schools. Public speaking teachers gave Cicero's speeches to pupils as examples to follow.

What Did Romans Wear?

Most people's clothes were made from wool. Wealthy people had clothes made from linen and silk.

Men's clothes

Men wore a knee-length tunic with short sleeves and a belt. Roman citizens wore a **toga** over their tunics. A toga was like a long sheet that they wound around their bodies, over the left shoulder, and under the right arm.

Women's clothes

Women wore a long tunic with another tunic, called a **stola**, on top. When they went out, they wore a cloak, called a palla.

Archaeologists found necklaces, gold rings, and hairpins. Gold came from Spain. Jewels came from Asia. Children wore amulets, small carved charms, or lockets. Parents believed amulets would keep children safe.

Statues tell a lot about Roman clothes. Men wore broaches to keep their togas in place.
Men and women wore sandals at home and soft boots when they went out. Poor people and slaves went barefoot.

Children's clothes

Boys wore a short tunic with a cloak. Girls wore an ankle-length tunic with a shawl or cloak.

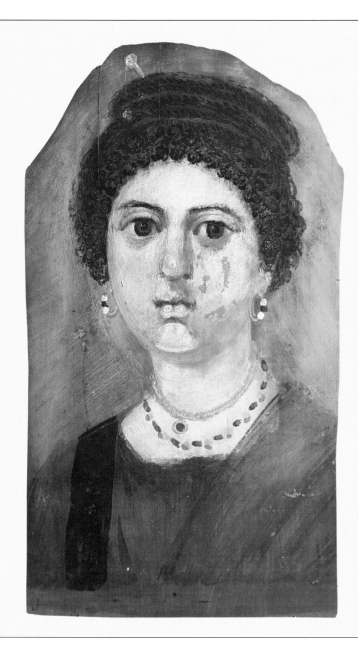

Hair styles

Wealthy women had very fancy hair styles. Their slaves styled their hair for them. Some women dyed their hair blonde. They bought blonde wigs and hairpieces. This is a Roman painting of a wealthy woman. She has a fancy hair style. Her earrings and necklaces are made from gold and precious stones.

Men's hair styles often followed that of the **emperor**. When the Emperor Hadrian grew a beard, hundreds of Roman men grew beards, too.

Family Life

A Roman family, or familia, was more than just the father, mother, and children. It included slaves, servants, grandparents, unmarried aunts and uncles, and the **household gods**. The father was the head of the family.

Weddings

Fathers arranged marriages for their children. Girls married when they were about 13. Boys married when they were a little older. The fathers signed a marriage contract at the bride's home. There were prayers and a special cake was offered to the gods and goddesses.

This gold wedding ring shows clasped hands. The carving above shows a wedding ceremony. The bride and groom hold hands. The bride says, "Where you are master, I am mistress."

Then the bride went in a torchlight procession to the groom's house. He carried her through the doorway because if she tripped, there would be bad luck.

Roman women kept their own property, but they were supposed to obey their husbands. A couple could divorce if they did not want to live together any more.

Roman names

When a baby was a few days old, it was shown to the father. If the father took the baby in his arms, the child was named and given a locket called a bulla. A baby had three names. The first was its own name, for example, Julia. The second was the name of the **clan**, like Tullius, and the third was the name of the family itself, like Cicero.

This carving shows a father and his son. First, the father watches his son as a baby being fed and then holds him. As a little boy, the son plays with a toy cart pulled by a donkey. Children also played with hoops, dice, and dolls.

Going to School

Children learned important things at home. Their parents taught them to obey rules, to tell the truth, and to help other people. When their parents had visitors, children stayed up late to listen to adult conversation. Cato wrote a book about how he taught his son at home.

Children could go to school when they were seven. They learned to read and write in Latin and Greek. They wrote with a pointed stick called a **stylus**. They did math problems using beads on a frame called an **abacus**.

This girl is writing on a wooden board covered in wax. She is using a stylus. Sometimes girls from wealthy families stayed at school after they turned thirteen.

These boys are wearing outdoor shoes and warm clothes to go to school. The teacher is looking crossly at a boy who is late.

Most girls left school when they were thirteen. Boys went on to a grammaticus. There they learned about public speaking. They read Greek and Roman literature. Slaves made their books. The slaves copied the poems of Homer and Virgil on sheets of papyrus. These sheets were then glued together and rolled up into books.

Boys left school when they were sixteen. After school, boys of wealthy families could go to Athens, Greece. There they studied with the Greek **philosophers** or learned to become lawyers. Boys of poor families became **apprentices** and learned a trade or a craft.

When a boy's first beard grew, he went through a special ceremony to show he was now a man. He put his toys away and was allowed to wear a **toga**.

> **Roman numerals**
> The Romans used letters for numbers.
> for example:
>
> | | |
> |---|---|
> | I = 1 | V = 5 |
> | X = 10 | L = 50 |
> | C = 100 | D = 500 |
> | M = 1,000. | |
>
> The numbers between are written as a series of letters before or after the main number.
>
> | | |
> |---|---|
> | 4 = IV | 6 = VI |
> | 15 = XV | 56 = LVI |
>
> MCMXCIX = 1999

Gods and Goddesses

The Romans believed in many gods and goddesses. They believed that if they pleased the gods, the gods would give them good luck. Romans thought that when they died, the god Mercury led their spirits into the **underworld** where gods and goddesses ruled.

The Romans worshiped the gods of the people that they conquered. They worshiped the gods of the Greeks. They worshiped Mithras from Persia, who gave courage. They worshiped Isis from Egypt, who promised life after death. The Romans followed many different religions and cults. But in Britain, where **druid priests sacrificed** people and animals, Romans were not allowed to become druids.

This tomb carving shows a procession of mourners. They are taking their loved one who has died to a burial ground. Sometimes the dead were buried or **cremated** with their belongings. Families remembered their dead at special, yearly festivals.

When the **emperor** Augustus died, the Roman **Senate** said he had become a god. Christians refused to worship Augustus. So the Romans persecuted them. The Romans killed thousands of Christians for their beliefs. Then, 300 years after the death of Jesus Christ, Emperor Constantine made Christianity the official religion of the Roman **Empire**.

The gods on this carving are, from left to right, Hercules, Minerva, Bacchus, Jupiter, Ceres, Juno, and Mercury.

Roman Gods   Romans and Greeks believed in many of the same gods. The Greek name follows the Roman name. Jupiter (Zeus) was god of the sky and king of all gods. His wife Juno (Hera) was goddess of women and mothers. All the gods were part of their family.

Mars (Ares) god of war; Ceres (Demeter) goddess of farming; Venus (Aphrodite) goddess of love and beauty; Minerva (Athena) goddess of crafts and wisdom; Mercury (Hermes) messenger of the gods; Diana (Artemis) goddess of the moon and hunting; Neptune (Poseidon) god of the sea; Vulcan (Hephaestus) god of the fire; Vesta (Hestia) goddess of the hearth; Bacchus (Dionysius) god of wine; Saturn (Kronos) god of farming; Janus god of doorways and journeys; Apollo (Apollo) god of light and music

Temples and Shrines

Romans built **temples** as homes for their gods and goddesses. Inside each temple, there was a **shrine** with a statue of the god or goddess. **Priests** made **sacrifices** in front of these statues. On special days, Romans sacrificed animals outside the temples. It was important to get everything right, or the gods would be angry.

Priests looked for signs, or omens, from the gods. Thunder and lightening were bad omens. Romans never did anything if the omens were bad. People went to **augurs** and astrologers to find out the future. The services of augurs and astrologers were expensive, so poor people went to **soothsayers.**

This temple is in Nimes, France. Nimes was once part of the Roman Empire. These columns are copied from columns found in Greek temples.

The Romans used five kinds of columns in their important buildings.

The Romans believed that the **household gods** helped them in their everyday lives. They believed the **lares** protected the home and the **penates** provided the family's food.

The Romans put small statues of the household gods on an altar in front of the fire or in the courtyard of a house. People prayed to these gods when they woke up and when they left the house.

Medicine and healing

Romans thought illness was a punishment from the gods. They made sacrifices so the gods would cure an illness. The Romans began to learn about medicine from the Greeks. Archaeologists have found medical instruments like the ones in the picture. Stone carvings show doctors at work. Eye infections were a common problem. One carving shows an eye doctor treating a patient. Doctors sold ointments made from herbs. Pliny wrote about a mustard gargle which was good for stomach upsets. Roman doctors charged high prices, so poor people often went to a chemist first.

23

A Roman Farm

In early times, most Romans worked on their own small farms. During long years of war, the men were away fighting. Women and children struggled to keep the farms going. Some farms were given to army commanders as rewards for battle victories. Slaves worked their land. By about 100 B.C. nearly all farming was done on large estates.

The photograph is an aerial view of a large Roman farm at Estrees-sur-Noye in northern France. The drawing shows what **archaeologists** think the estate looked like in Roman times.

The *vilicus* lived in a smaller villa with small rooms for the slaves.

Some farm workers lived in slaves' quarters around the courtyard, near the cattle, pigs and hens they looked after.

Storehouses

Gardens separate the main villa from the rest of the farm.

Some buildings in the courtyard would have been used as stables and cowsheds. One would have been a mill for grinding grain, and another a spinning and weaving room.

Main gate

Owners and managers

The owners of large farms were very
wealthy. They lived in cities for most of the
year. They only visited their farms in the
summer, when it was too hot to be in the
cities. Then, they stayed in a villa, which is a
large house on the farm estate. A manager,
called a vilicus, and a housekeeper, called
the vilica, ran the farm. Slaves did the
farm work.

Buildings and plants

Archaeologists have found Roman farm sites
all over Europe and North Africa. From
pieces of stone, brick, and tiles, they can tell
what the buildings were like. From seeds
and vegetable remains, they can tell what
crops were grown.

In Italy, farmers grew vines, olives, and corn.
Farms in Britain and France grew wheat,
barley, beans, peas, plums, and apples. The
Romans brought new plants, such as
cabbages, carrots, cherries, and walnuts to
Britain.

The big farms had gardens around the villa.
The Romans planted hedges of yew, box,
and cypress. They planted trees to give
shade. They grew roses, lilies, and violets.

The Farming Year

Festivals

Each part of the farming year had a special festival. The Romans offered gifts to the gods before plowing the land and sowing seeds. In May, every farm worker walked around the fields in a special procession asking the gods to help the crops ripen. In the fall, Romans celebrated the harvest with sports and feasts.

Running the farm

A farm estate was like a small town. It provided everything the farm workers needed. The vilicus and vilica were slaves. They had great responsibilities and worked hard.

Archaeologists found this **mosaic** in Carthage in North Africa. It was probably made in the 4th century A.D. It shows a boar hunt. The Romans also hunted deer. They caught partridges, pheasants, and pigeons.

This mosaic shows slaves picking and pressing grapes to make wine. Romans grew enough grapes to make wine both for themselves and to sell to other countries.

Archaeologists found these Roman farm tools at Newstead on the Tweed River in Scotland. The scythe is made from iron. The rake on the right is made from the horns of a red deer.

Slaves made cheese from cow's and goat's milk. They looked after chickens, ducks, and geese. They collected honey from bees. They pressed olives for oil and ground grain into flour. They made woolen cloth.

The Roman calendar
Romans named some of their months after gods and goddesses: January (Janus), March (Mars), May (Maia), and June (Juno). February was from the name of a special ceremony. April meant "the opening of flowers." Julius Caesar named July after himself. Augustus did the same with August. Until 46 B.C., the Roman year started on the first day of March.

A Town in the Empire

Archaeologists have found Roman cities all over its vast **empire**. Some, like Volubis in Algeria, are in ruins, but no one has built over them. Some Roman cities, like Bath in England, have been built over for hundreds of years.

Beginnings

Some Roman towns began as forts where soldiers lived. Others began as new towns in conquered lands.

Thamugadi, now called Timgad in Algeria, North Africa, was built in A.D. 100 for Roman soldiers.

Town planning

Romans planned their cities on a grid system. The streets were straight and crossed each other at right angles. The roads divided the towns into squares.

Water

The Romans built **aqueducts** to carry water from lakes and rivers to their towns. Aqueducts carried water on a bridge across a valley or in pipes underground. Romans knew that clean water was important.

Builders

Materials

Romans used stone and brick in their buildings. They invented a type of concrete in about 200 B.C.

Arches

Romans used arches to hold up **aqueducts**, bridges, and tall buildings. They knew that squeezing an arch, which is a semicircle, against a central keystone is the strongest shape. It can carry the weight of a wall or hold up a roof.

These are carvings on Trajan's Column. It was built in A.D. 114 by the **Emperor** Trajan to celebrate a great victory. In the top row, soldiers are building stone fortifications. Fortificaions were used to protect the soldiers during a battle.

Workers

Roman engineers, surveyors, and masons went all over the **empire** showing people how to build. The Romans used hundreds of slaves to build their projects.

Roman Roads

The Romans built 53,000 miles (85,000 kilometers) of roads to all parts of their empire. Surveyors who travelled with the Roman army planned the roads. First, surveyors worked out the most direct route. Then soldiers and slaves dug a wide trench along this route. They filled the trench with layers of sand, concrete, small stones and stone blocks. Roman roads were very strong. The routes of Roman roads are still part of the road system in Britain and Europe.

This is a Roman aqueduct in Segovia, Spain. The two layers of arches carried water 118 feet (36 meters) above the streets. Romans looked for a lake or river that was higher than the town. Then they built an aqueduct that sloped gently downhill to the town. They lined the water channel with concrete to keep the water from leaking.

Inside a Town House

Archaeologists dug in the volcanic ash and mud that covered Pompeii and Herculaneum. They found houses with furniture and pots and pans. From this, much is known about how the Romans lived in town houses.

Most town houses had central heating. Hot air from a furnace went through channels under the floor and through pipes in the walls. Some people had their own baths.

The *atrium* or main hall had a hole in the roof to let in light. A water tank or ornamental pool called an *impluvium* caught rainwater which came through the hole.

The *tablinium* was a study or private library.

The courtyard had flower borders and a covered passage around the outside.

The *lararium* or shrine to the household gods.

The dining room or *triclinium*.

Entrance passage

tablinium

peristyle

lararium

courtyard

bedrooms

atrium

impluvium

entrance

triclinium

kitchen

shops

bedrooms

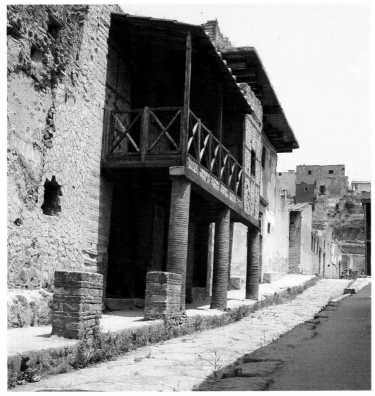

This street is in Herculaneum. Two families lived in these houses. One family lived on the upper floor, and the other family lived on the ground floor. In Rome, poorer people lived in apartment buildings. There were one-room schools and carry-out restaurants in the apartment buildings.

Furniture

Roman furniture was made from wood. Most of it has now rotted away. Wall paintings tell us something about what was in their homes.

Romans had beds, chairs, stools, and tables. They had wooden cupboards and chests in which they kept their books, clothes, and food. They had lamps that burned olive oil and candles made from reeds coated in wax.

Romans painted pictures on the walls of their houses. This one is in a house near Pompeii.

Cooking and Eating

Early Romans ate very simply until they got new ideas about food from conquered lands. The first Romans did not bake bread. They ate boiled meat and a kind of soup.

Mealtimes

Later Romans ate a breakfast of bread and cheese. Lunch was a cold meal of bread, meat, and fruit. The most important meal was dinner at about 4:00 in the afternoon. Roast meats, fish, fruit, and dessert were served. When there were guests, dinner lasted into the night.

A Roman kitchen might have looked like this. Wealthy people would have had slaves to cook food on charcoal stoves. Poor people cooked food in the streets or in a local baker's oven.

A feast

Romans lay on couches to eat. They ate with their fingers and with knives and spoons. Slaves served the meal and brought bowls of water and towels for people to wash their hands during a meal.

A feast had many courses. Romans ate shellfish, fish, wild boar, roast pheasant, partridge, peacocks, ostriches, fruit, and sweets. They drank wine, which they sometimes mixed with water or honey. Some of what we know about Roman food comes from a recipe book written by Marcus Apicius.

This **mosaic** shows the fish eaten by the Romans.

Between courses, the guests had serious conversations and discussions. There was usually some sort of musical entertainment. Slaves played musical instruments like harps and a type of harp called a **cithara**. They played panpipes and trumpets. Slave girls danced to the music.

Many Roman writers said that wealthy people ate too much and spent too much money on food. Pliny the Younger wrote that he went to feasts because he liked the conversation.

This mosaic was found in Cicero's villa at Pompeii. It shows street entertainers playing music and dancing.

At the Baths

Wealthy people had baths in their own homes. Poorer people went to public baths in the town. They were not expensive and in some towns, they were free. Most Romans enjoyed going to the baths. They relaxed there and chatted with friends.

There were more than 900 public baths in Rome. Men finished work at about 3:00 in the afternoon and then went to the baths. They would spend an hour there before going home for dinner. Women could only use the baths in the morning when the men were not there.

The Great Bath at Aquae Sulis is in western England. The British town is now called Bath. This great bath was filled with water that flowed from a hot spring. People thought the water cured illnesses.

Bathing and exercise kept the Romans fit and healthy. First, a slave rubbed oil into the bather's body. Then the bather went into the tepidarium where there were two baths of warm water. Next, the bather went into a very hot bath called a caldarium. The room was full of steam and made the bather sweat. The bather used a strigil to scrape oil and dirt off his or her skin, and then the bather plunged into a cold bath called a frigidarium. Finally, a slave rubbed scented oil into the bather's skin.

Several Roman baths still stand today. However, the large Caracalla Baths in Rome were destroyed by invading Goths three hundred years after they were built. These baths, built between A.D. 206 and 235, could be used by 1,600 bathers at a time.

Public Holidays

The Romans did not have weekends off work, as most people do nowadays. Instead, they had 120 days of public holidays throughout the year. On these holidays, Romans watched plays or listened to concerts. They went to the **amphitheater** to watch chariot races and gladiator fights.

Gladiators

Gladiators were slaves or criminals who were trained to fight. They fought each other or wild animals. They fought to the death in front of huge crowds.

Chariot races

Most towns had a special racetrack for chariot races. Hundreds of people came to watch. The Circus Maximus in Rome held 250 thousand people.

Gladiators wore armor and a helmet. They fought with swords or a three-pronged spear. This amphitheater at El Djem, Tunisia, in Africa, had underground cages to hold wild animals that gladiators would fight.

Chariot racing was very dangerous. The drivers bumped and rammed each other. Chariots were often knocked over. The charioteers wore helmets and leather chest and leg protectors. Even so, they were sometimes hurt or killed.

Four teams of chariots raced against each other. Two or four horses pulled each chariot. Each team wore a different color. The crowd cheered for their favorite team. Each race was seven laps of the stadium, which was about 4 miles (6.5 kilometers).

At the theater

Roman theaters were in the open air. People sat on stone seats arranged in a semi-circle around the stage. Some theaters held more than 7,000 people. The actors wore large masks because the audience was too far away to see their faces. Some masks were sad, and some were happy.

Crafts and Craftworkers

When Rome was a **republic**, the **plebeians** were craftworkers and tradesmen. By the end of the republic in 27 B.C., wealthy landowners had slaves working their farms. These slaves took over the crafts from the plebeians. Many plebeian craftworkers moved to the towns.

City craftworkers

Craftworkers had their own workshops. They sold their goods from their workshops or in the local markets. Some craftworkers were helped by **apprentices** and slaves.

Goldsmiths, silversmiths, and jewelers made plates, goblets, and jewelry. Potters made clay pots, cups, and plates. Blacksmiths made tools, weapons, and pots and pans from iron. Carpenters carved furniture and farm tools from wood. Cobblers made boots and sandals. Leatherworkers made belts and shields for soldiers.

Raw materials

Craftworkers need raw materials with which to work. Jewelers imported emeralds and amethysts from China.

This wall painting of a potter's workshop is from Pompeii.
Potters made tiles as well as pots. A workman scratched "I made 550 tiles" on a piece of Roman pottery. Another worker added "And I smashed 51." Both workers wrote in Latin.

Archaeologists have found Roman jars, bottles, bowls, and drinking glasses made from glass. Romans learned how to make glass from craftworkers in Syria.

Glass objects like these were difficult to make. They were very expensive.

Metalworkers got their gold and silver from Spain and Greece. Tin came from Britain. Copper came from Italy, Cyprus, and Spain. Miners worked underground. It was hot, dark, cramped, airless, and very dangerous.

Shops

Markets

Every city had a **forum**. This was the main market place as well as the place from where the city was governed. Rome had a big weekly market as well as smaller markets near the forum. These markets opened every day. They sold fruit, vegetables, meat, fish, and cloth.

Shops

The streets around the forum were crowded with shops. There were butchers, bakers, grocers, barbers, booksellers, and cloth sellers. At Pompeii, **archaeologists** have found shops with stone counters facing the street. Shops were run by families and worked by slaves.

Archaeologists have found many stone carvings of shops that show us what they looked like and what they sold. This is a carving of a butcher's shop.
In wealthy families, slaves shopped for food. In other families, this job was usually done by men.

Buying and selling

Merchants and bankers had their offices in the forum. Merchants became rich by **importing** and **exporting** goods. They borrowed money from bankers to run their businesses. Bankers charged the merchants money for the loans. This was how bankers made their money.

Inspectors

Government inspectors visited markets and shops to check that food was accurately weighed and priced. They checked for quality, too.

This coin is a bronze sestertii. It has the head of **Emperor** Nero on one side.
Four sestertii were worth one silver denarii, and twenty five denarii were worth one gold aurei.

This bakery was in Pompeii. Flour was ground in the mill on the right. The bakers lit a fire in the bottom part of the oven on the left. The bread was baked in the top part.

Transportation

Coins and pottery

Archaeologists have found Roman coins in many different countries. This tells us that the Romans traded in countries far from Rome. Roman ships carried oil, flour, and wine in large pottery jars called **amphorae**. Archaeologists can often match found bits of pottery with workshops far away.

Wrecks

Archaeologists study wrecks of ships and their cargoes. They can tell where the ships came from and where they were going.

Trade in the empire

Archaeologists found this **mosaic** of ships and dolphins in Ostia. Ostia was a city at the mouth of the Tiber River. Large merchant ships anchored there. Then smaller ships took the goods to warehouses.

Ships

It was cheaper to carry goods by sea than overland. Roman ships had sails and oars to use if there was no wind. Roman ships carried wheat and wine, silks, and spices. It took two to three weeks for a cargo ship to sail from Egypt to Rome.

Land travel

Some people preferred to travel by land. They were afraid of shipwrecks and pirates. Most Roman roads were safe, although there were some bandits. There were inns along main roads where travelers could stay over night. Government messengers changed their horses at these inns. They rode fast, carrying messages all over the **empire**. Ordinary people walked or rode donkeys and mules.

Transportation included animals pulling carts.

War with Carthage

By 290 B.C., the Romans were a strong force. They had defeated many of the people living on their borders. They had bribed other tribes to keep away.

War at Sea

The Romans began to look for lands beyond their borders. This led to many years of war with the Carthaginians. These people came from the wealthy trading state of Carthage in North Africa. The Romans and the Carthaginians quarreled over Sicily, an island in the Mediterranean Sea. They both wanted to control the island's ports and wheat fields. The Romans built a fleet of warships. They defeated the Carthaginians at sea in 241 B.C.

Roman warships carried 400 soldiers. Roman ships attacked enemy ships by first ramming a huge spike into their sides. This fastened the ships together. Then Roman soldiers jumped onto the enemy ship and fought hand-to-hand.

War on land

The Carthaginian general Hannibal made a plan to attack Rome. He marched his army 1,200 miles (1,931 kilometers) and invaded Italy. The Carthaginians defeated a Roman army at Trebbia. A year later, they defeated the Romans at Lake Trasimene. Hannibal's army killed 70,000 Roman soldiers. Then his army marched south to Cannae, where again they defeated the Romans.

The Roman general, Scipio, decided to attack Carthaginian colonies. He conquered Spain in 207 B.C. and invaded North Africa. Hannibal rushed back to defend Carthage. At Zama, in 202 B.C., Scipio defeated Hannibal's army. Hannibal escaped back to Carthage and made peace with Rome.

This coin has a portrait of Hannibal on one side and an elephant on the other. He was very young when he became a general, but even so, he nearly beat the Romans.

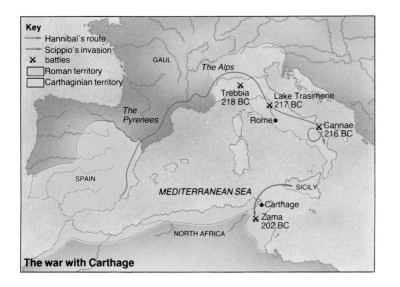

Key
— Hannibal's route
— Scippio's invasion
✗ battles
☐ Roman territory
☐ Carthaginian territory

GAUL
The Alps
The Pyrenees
Trebbia 218 BC
Lake Trasimene 217 BC
Rome
Cannae 216 BC
SPAIN
MEDITERRANEAN SEA
SICILY
Carthage
Zama 202 BC
NORTH AFRICA

The war with Carthage

Hannibal marched for five months with his army of 60,000 men and 37 elephants. It took 15 days to cross the Alps Mountains on the way to Italy. Forty thousand men died.

Legionaries and Centurions

The first Roman armies were made up of ordinary **citizens**. Young men were called up to fight a war. Older men cleaned weapons and defended their city. Then, in 107 B.C., everything changed. Marius, who was a very smart general, became **consul**. He knew the army needed well-trained men who could fight. He planned a new army.

The Roman army

Men joined for twenty years as full-time soldiers. They were paid about 255 denarii a year, which was a good living. Roman soldiers were trained to march, fight, and build roads and bridges.

A standard bearer
Each **legion** had a standard. This was a pole with a silver eagle on the top and the legion's badges below. In battle, the standard was used to signal to the soldiers who were marching behind it.

A legionary
He wore an iron helmet and a metal cuirass to protect his body. His kilt was made from strips of leather and metal. He fought with a short sword, a dagger, and a long spear. He carried a leather shield.

The army was divided into legions of about 6,000 men. Each legion was made up of ten **cohorts**. In each cohort, there were six centuries of about 100 men. Each legion also had a troop of about 700 cavalry.

Legionaries were ordinary soldiers. A legionary could become a **centurion**, who commanded a century. A legate commanded a legion. Below him were six senior officers called **tribunes**.

By 27 B.C., there were 28 legions. The soldiers lived in forts all over the **empire**.

Archaeologists have found Roman armor and weapons in all the Roman forts throughout the empire. Metal objects last a long time. They do not break into little pieces when buried underground.

A centurion
He wore a fancy helmet and a cloak over his cuirass. He wore greaves to protect his legs. He wore breeches in cold climates.

War!

Roman soldiers had to be fit. They had to carry all their own equipment when they marched. They also had to carry clothes, tents, food, and cooking pots. An army could march about 21 miles (34 km) a day. Slaves went with the Roman army to help with the work.

Romans made many stone carvings of their battles. They made them on columns and arches that were built in memory of a famous victory. The carvings on **Emperor Trajan's** column, built in A.D. **114**, show details of Roman weapons, armor, and battle tactics.

This picture of Roman soldiers was painted long after Roman times. The artist had studied Roman siege warfare.

Pontoon bridges

Roman armies crossed deep rivers on pontoon bridges. They made rafts of wood and tied them together. These rafts stretched from one bank to the other.

Camps

Each night the army set up camp. They dug a ditch and made earth walls to protect the camp from attack.

Siege warfare

The Romans pushed a moveable attack tower toward the enemy's walls. Soldiers on top of the tower hurled spears into the town. When the tower was close to the walls, a drawbridge was lowered. Then the soldiers swarmed across it into the town.

Defending a town

It was difficult to attack a strongly defended town. The town walls were made from thick stone and the doors from heavy wood. Soldiers stood on top of the town walls with spears to hurl and arrows to fire at the attackers. But, the Romans had ways of overcoming this and laying siege to a defended town.

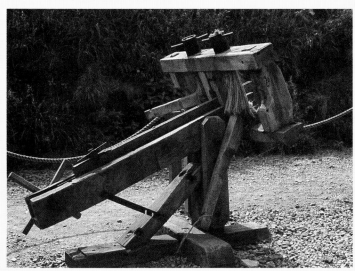

The Romans used a giant catapult called a ballista to hurl stones. Some catapults could throw stones weighing about 88 pounds (40 kilograms). This is a photograph of a ballista. It was built in modern times from a description written by Vitruvius, a Roman architect and engineer.

Wars in Italy

Quarrels between different groups of people in Italy led to civil war.

Tiberius and Gaius

Wealthy men bought land and set up farms that they worked with slaves. **Plebeians** were forced off the land. In the towns, there was no work for them. Then in 133 B.C., Tiberius was elected **tribune**. He had a plan to rent land to the plebeians, but land-owning Romans refused to give up any of their land. Tiberius and 300 of his supporters were murdered. Tiberius' brother Gaius was elected tribune in 123 B.C. He said the Senate should buy wheat and sell it cheaply to poor people. He said that all the people should be Roman **citizens**, not just the people of Rome. He was murdered, too.

Civil War

In 91 B.C., the plebians rebelled. The **Senate** sent two generals, Marius and Sulla, to fight them. Many people died. In 90 B.C., the Senate promised to let all the people be Roman citizens. Then Sulla and Marius fought each other. The fighting went on until 82 B.C., when Sulla won control of the Senate.

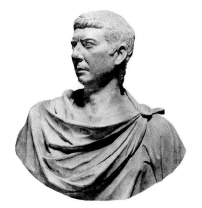

The Romans were successful conquerors because of their army. Pompey brought great treasures back to Rome.

The people supported Julius Caesar because he was a good general, like Pompey.

The end of the republic

In 70 B.C., Pompey, Sulla's brilliant and popular general, became a **consul**.

In 59 B.C., Julius Caesar was elected consul. He became governor of southern Gaul, which is now France, and gradually brought northern Gaul under Roman rule. Pompey was jealous of Caesar. He got the Senate to order Caesar to resign his command. Caesar refused and marched into Rome with his army. Pompey fled to Greece where his army was defeated by Caesar's army. Pompey escaped to Egypt where he was murdered. Caesar returned to Rome in triumph. He ruled Rome as a dictator. Some senators hated this, and in 44 B.C. they murdered him.

Spartacus was an escaped slave. He led a revolt of 70,000 slaves. In 71 B.C., Marcus Crassus led an army against the slaves. Spartacus was killed, and thousand of his supporters were crucified along the Appian Way. The story of Spartacus has been made into a ballet and a movie. This is a photograph of a scene from the ballet.

The Emperors

Octavian and Mark Antony

Octavian was Caesar's adopted son and heir. He and Mark Antony, a supporter of Caesar, tracked down Caesar's murderers. They killed the leaders, Cassius and Brutus. Then Octavian and Mark Antony divided the **empire** between them. Mark Antony ruled Egypt and the East. Octavian ruled Italy and the West.

Mark Antony fell in love with Cleopatra, the Queen of Egypt. Octavian was angry with Mark Antony for neglecting his empire, and they went to war. Their two war fleets met off the coast of Greece. Octavian's fleet won, and Mark Antony and Cleopatra killed themselves. Octavian returned to Rome in triumph. The **Senate** agreed that Octavian should become the first Roman **emperor**.

The Arch of Titus stands in the Forum in Rome. Titus was emperor from A.D. 79–81. He commanded the army that put down a Jewish revolt in Judea. The arch shows Roman soldiers carrying away Jewish treasure.

The Roman emperors

Augustus (27 B.C.–A.D. 14) did not try to gain new lands because he thought the empire was big enough. He chose the **provincial** governors and paid officials to help them. He built roads to link the provinces. He encouraged music and writing.

The next four emperors were all related to Augustus, but none of them ruled as well as he did.

Tiberius (A.D. 14–37) made the empire stronger, but became a tyrant later in his rule.

Caligula (A.D. 37–41) carried on Tiberius' reign of terror and was probably crazy. He made his horse a **consul** and built a special palace for it.

Emperor Augustus

Claudius (A.D. 41–54) began the conquest of Britain.

Nero (A.D. 54–68) In A.D. 64, a great fire destroyed part of Rome. Nero blamed the Christians and had many of them killed. Eventually, his cruelty turned the people against him, and he killed himself.

After Nero, the emperor was usually a general. Under the reign of Trajan (A.D. 98–117), the empire reached its greatest size.

Augustus

Octavian changed his name to Augustus. He brought peace to the empire and made Rome a beautiful city. Augustus ruled as emperor until A.D. 14. Before he died, he chose his successor. Now the Roman people could not vote for their leader.

A Roman Province

Augustus took control of the whole **empire**. He set up a new system of governing the **provinces**. Each governor was in charge for three to five years. He was paid a salary and had officials to help him. He had to send reports back to Rome, collect taxes, and hear legal cases. Soldiers helped him keep control.

The conquest of Britain

Julius Caesar invaded Britain in 55 B.C. But storms wrecked some of his ships, and his cavalry could not cross the sea to Britain. He tried again in 54 B.C. This time he had 800 ships, 25,000 soldiers, and 2,000 cavalry. The Romans won battles against the local tribes. They made the conquered people send gifts to Rome.

Hadrian's Wall crossed Britain from east to west. It was 75 miles (121 km) long, 20 feet (6 m) high, and 10 feet (3 m) wide. About 14,000 soldiers manned the wall. They lived in forts and kept watch from towers and gatehouses.

Archaeologists excavated a Roman palace at Fishbourne, in Sussex, England. This is one of the palace's **mosaic** floors.

Then Caesar and his army left. They were back in Rome before winter.

The Romans invaded Britain again in A.D. 43. Then **Emperor** Claudius conquered eastern and southern Britain. The British fought on in the north and west until their king, Caratacus, was defeated by the Romans in A.D. 51. In A.D. 78, Julius Agricola became governor of the province of Britannia, or Britain.

Life in Roman Britain

Britain became a more peaceful province of Rome. The Romans built **temples,** inns, and **amphitheaters** outside the walls of their forts. The soldiers moved on to defend the frontiers of the empire, like Hadrian's Wall. Then, the workshops, hospitals, bath houses, and other fort buildings became part of the town that surrounded them.

The Romans taught the British people how to build homes from stone and towns with straight streets. Some Romans married British women. They and their children and grandchildren lived like Romans. They spoke Latin, had Roman furniture in their houses, and wore **togas**.

The Emperor Hadrian spent 15 years traveling around his empire. He ordered walls, ditches, and forts to be built to protect the borders of the empire from invaders. In Britain, he ordered a wall to be built from the Irish Sea to the North Sea. He wanted to stop tribes in Scotland from attacking the province.

The Fall of Rome

Tribes living outside the Roman **empire** began attacking it. The Romans had to send more and more soldiers to defend the frontiers of their empire. Taxes had to be increased to pay for them. People did not want to pay higher taxes. Everywhere there was unrest. The army split and supported the claims of different men to be **emperor**. Between A.D. 211 and 284, twenty emperors were murdered.

The government of the empire was in chaos. Then, in A.D. 410 and again in A.D. 476, the Goths, a Germanic tribe, invaded Italy and captured Rome. It was the end of the empire in the west. The Eastern Empire lasted until it was captured by the Muslims in A.D. 1453.

In A.D. 284, the large Roman Empire was ruled by both Diocletian and Maximianus. Diocletian ruled the Eastern Empire, and Maximianus ruled the Western Empire. When they retired, civil war broke out.

The Romans called all tribes outside their empire "barbarians." In A.D. 376, hordes of barbarians began invading the Roman Empire. Within 100 years, the "barbarians" ruled the Western Empire.

58

The legacy of Rome

The barbarian invaders destroyed many Roman towns and left them in ruins. People forgot the Roman ways.

However, Rome remained the center of Christianity, and the Latin language was used in church services. It became the basis of most modern European languages and of government and law.

In the 15th century, a new age began. It was called the renaissance, or rebirth. Scholars and artists rediscovered the architecture and writings of Rome and Greece. This rediscovery has inspired people ever since.

Today, the Pope is head of the Catholic Church and lives in Vatican City in Rome. After the fall of the empire, Rome stayed the center of the Christian Church. The Pope's **priests** spread Christianity throughout the barbarian tribes who had taken over the Western Empire. Latin stayed as the official language of the Church for hundreds of years.

Time Line

B.C.

753	The founding of Rome
509	Tarquin the Proud, the last king of Rome, is driven out. Rome becomes a **republic.**
494	The **plebians** are given the right to choose their own **tribunes.**
264	The First Punic War begins. Romans build their first warships and learn to fight at sea.
218	The Second Punic War begins. Hannibal marches across the Alps.
149	The Third Punic War begins. Carthage destroyed by the Romans. North Africa becomes a Roman **province.**
133	Tiberius becomes tribune of the people.
123	Gaius becomes tribune of the people.
107	Marius becomes **consul** and sets up a new army.
91	The plebians rebel.
82	Sulla rules as a dictator.
73–1	Spartacus leads a slaves' revolt. Spartacus is killed and the slaves' revolt is defeated.
58–49	Julius Caesar conquers Gaul and invades Britain twice.
44	Julius Caesar is murdered.
43	Mark Antony and Octavian take power.
31	Battle of Actium: Octavian defeats Mark Antony.
27	Octavian becomes Augustus, the first **emperor.**

A.D.

14	Tiberius becomes emperor.
37	Caligula becomes emperor.
41	Claudius becomes emperor.
43	Claudius invades Britain.
64	A great fire destroys most of Rome.
79	Vesuvius erupts and destroys Pompeii and Herculaneum.
80	Emperor Titus opens the Colosseum in Rome.
114	Trajan's column is built in Rome.
122–126	Hadrian's Wall is built in northern Britain.
252	Barbarian tribes begin to invade the empire.
306	Constantine becomes emperor.
313	Christianity becomes the official religion of the Roman Empire.
395	The Roman Empire is divided into two halves.
410	The Germanic tribe of Goths attack Rome.
445	The Teutonic tribe of Vandals attack Rome.
476	The Western Empire is defeated by the Goths.
1453	The Eastern Empire is defeated by the Muslims.

Glossary

abacus wooden frame with rows of beads on wires used for counting

amphitheater oval-shaped building with rows of seats around a central space where fights or games were held

amphorae large, clay storage jar

apprentice someone who learns a trade by working with someone who is an expert

aqueduct sloping bridge or channel, often built on arches, for carrying water overland to towns

archaeologist person who finds out what happened in the past by **excavating** old buildings and objects

augur religious person

centurion leader of 100 soldiers

cithara small musical instrument

citizen person who lives in a city and chooses its rulers

clan group of related families that share an ancestor

cohort group of 600 men in the army

consuls two men elected for one year to be in charge of law and order in Rome

cremate to burn a dead body

druid follower of an old British religion

emperor ruler of an **empire**

empire group of countries under the rule of one country

excavate to dig in the ground to uncover buildings and objects

forum public meeting place

household gods gods that are special to one family

lares Roman household gods that protected the outside of the home

legion largest unit in the Roman army of four to six thousand soldiers led by a legate

legionary foot soldier

magistrate person who makes laws and sees that they are carried out

mosaic pieces of glass, stone, or wood put together to form a picture or design

noble person born into an important family; the group of nobles in a country is called the nobility

patrician wealthy Roman **citizen**

penates Roman household gods that protected the inside of the home

philosopher person who studies the meaning of life

plebeian: any Roman **citizen** who was not a **patrician**

priest man who performs all the duties and the ceremonies for worshipping the gods

province part of a country or **empire** ruled by a governor

republic country or group of countries where the people elect the government

sacrifice to kill an animal or person as an offering to the gods

Senate the group of about 300 Romans who advised the **magistrates**

shrine holy place

soothsayer person who uses magic to predict future events

stola loose robe worn by women

stylus pointed tool used to write

temple building or place where people worship their god or gods

toga loose garment worn by Roman **citizens**

tribune man who represented the **plebeians**

underworld place where the spirits of the dead went

More Books to Read

Corbishley, Mike. *Everyday Life in Roman Times.* Danbury, Conn: Franklin Watts, 1994.

Guittard, Charles. *The Romans: Life in the Empire.* Brookfield, Conn: Millbrook Press, 1992.

MacDonald, Fiona. *So You Want to Be a Roman Soldier.* Brookfield, Conn: Millbrook Press, 1994.

Shuter, Jane. *The Ancient Romans.* Des Plaines, IL: Heinemann Interactive Library, 1998.

Whittock, Martyn. *The Roman Empire.* New York: Peter Bedrick, 1996.

Index